CURTISHIA WILLIAMS STARLING

POSITIONED

CURTISHIA WILLIAMS STARLING

POSITIONED

POSITIONED
Copyright © 2021 by Curtishia Williams Starling
ISBN: 978-1-7367455-5-7
All Rights Reserved. No part of this publication may be reproduced, distributed, or transmitted in any form or by any means, including photocopying, recording, or other electronic or mechanical methods, without the prior written permission of the publisher, except certain other noncommercial uses permitted by copyright law. All quotes are cited within the content, reference by the author, or are unknown and are not being credited to the work of any contributing author of this book. No portion of this work is meant to defame anyone but is based on my personal life's experiences.
Cover by Design Place LLC
Edited by Shawn Jackson
Published by One2Mpower Publishing LLC

Acknowledgments

God created me with the ending in mind. This has shaped my inspiration for writing this book. First, I would like to thank my Lord and Savior, Jesus Christ, for all that He has done, is doing, and will do for me, my family, and others. It is by His grace and mercy that I can do what I love.

There are several people that have encouraged me along the way, but I must pinpoint the church member that I'm sure has no idea that she was a huge success in encouraging me. She spoke a very simple message to her sister in response to a message that I shared. Her words were, "That girl has a way with words. She should be leading!" Somehow, I overlooked the leading part but focused on the portion of having a way with words. I have been talking about writing a book for years now, and her words gave me the confidence to DO IT.

My wonderful husband, Everett Starling, who is always "team Curtishia," inspired me to live my dream, supports me in any way needed, and covered me in prayer daily. My father, Curtis Williams, who is looking down from heaven, inspired this book. The time spent with him was short-lived on earth but lives in my heart forever.

POSITIONED

My amazing, strong mother, Mozella Pennic, who raised me to believe I can do anything and never gave up on me regardless of the obstacles faced.

My awesome son, Lekwameh (Kwameh) Lewis, has been a huge inspiration in my life that motivates me daily and supports any out-of-the-box idea I present. I am beyond grateful to have such a handsome, intelligent, resilient, and cultivated son alongside. To my bonus kids: Tomeka, Jamarques, Everett Jr., Hilton, and Mason, thank you for the encouragement and love given to me. I'm grateful for my supportive sisters, brothers, friends, nieces, nephews, cousins, aunts and uncle that never turned their backs on me.

My friend, Mataya Wright Williams, has been a huge influence on this journey. Seeing her live out her dream gave me the courage to follow mine. I am grateful for the people that caused hurt, pain, and discord on this journey because, without them, there would be no story. I am grateful for all the people that placed labels on my identity to reflect ghetto, drunk, single mother, project girl, crazy, uncanny, loud, etc. because, without you, the search for my purpose would fail to exist. To every pastor that spoke life in me, inspired, transformed, and led with transparency, thank you!

Forewarning

If you purchased this book because you are searching for scholarly written material, I would like to be the first to apologize. The purpose of this book is to be easily read by any person regardless of age, educational background, and ethnicity that can identify or be helped by this story. My hope is to inspire others to live their dream, heal with freedom, and make a difference in their avenues traveled. I am not a mental health expert, nor do I hold any ill feelings towards the organizations mentioned. The illustrations are used solely to encourage others to remain on the course. The military has had a huge impact on my life, and I am beyond ecstatic and grateful for the opportunity to serve.

POSITIONED

Cool-Loo

The name Curtis Williams meant a lot to many people. In particular, me. Curtis Williams was my dad's name. My dad was a dark-skinned, humorous, handsome guy that everyone loved. Friends and family adored his presence. Dad said Merry Christmas to everyone every day. I never quite understood why he said those words daily, ate scrambled eggs every day with sliced tomatoes, or how he could find humor in any situation. He dressed sharp. My fondest memory was him sporting his long leather trench coat with his Stacy Adam shoes.

While attending Alabama State University on a football scholarship, my dad was drafted to the United States Army to fight during the Vietnam War. After returning from the Vietnam War, he worked as a butcher and later found a career in construction. My mother always told me my dad wanted a boy until he met me. He was so proud of me and grateful that I shared his name. Not only did I share his name, but he also gave me the nickname "Cool-Loo." It felt so good to know I was adored by my dad.

POSITIONED

I was truly my daddy's princess! You know the type you would see in the grocery store kicking and screaming because they did not get their way. Well, almost that, without the kicking and screaming. I was a "spoiled rotten child" because my dad bought me whatever I wanted and took me anywhere I wanted to go. Of all the places he would take me, my favorite one was going to the IGA Store. On Fridays, after work, dad would take me to the IGA Store and buy me whatever I wanted. As a child, this was a huge deal. I looked forward to doing it weekly. I always selected big bag of potato chips and ice cream. I felt like a true princess, and no one could ever tell me any different. After our weekly trip to the store, dad always said, "Don't have a boyfriend until you are twenty-five, and do not marry until thirty-five." We always laughed after he said that. I had no idea what any of it meant. I thought it was just another corny joke my dad was telling.

Heart Theft

One day, dad came home and was sitting in the bathroom fully clothed with the door open. He called for me. When I arrived in the bathroom, his skin was drenched in sweat. It looked as if he had been in the tub and sat up. Only his clothes were semi-dry. He asked me to go get some cold water out of the fridge and bring it to him. I went down the stairs to get the water and brought the whole jug to daddy. I felt he must be mighty thirsty, judging by the way he was sweating. Dad unbuttoned his shirt and asked me to throw the iced-cold water on his chest. I started crying, saying, "Daddy, the water is too cold. It is going to hurt you." He said, "No, Cool-Loo. It will make me cool down. Daddy really hot." With tears in my eyes, I did as he ordered. Dad did not flinch. It was as if the water was warm because he seemed unbothered. I screamed out to my mother, telling her that something was wrong with daddy. That water was too cold to hit anyone's skin.

The next week, my first-grade class was selected to perform at Dalraida Elementary School's Parent Teacher Association (PTA) Meeting. When I received the news, I rushed home to give dad the news. Dad was overjoyed;

he assured me he would be there. I asked if he could buy me a pink shirt, blue jean coveralls, pink chucks, and a new bookbag to match. He purchased all the items except the bookbag and said he would get it later. My mom and dad both attended my show. They told me how proud they were of me. I was so glad that my dad got to see me perform.

After the performance, I continued to call my dad to inquire about my bookbag he was going to buy me. After five times of asking, my dad made the comment, "Your mom is going to buy you whatever you want in the future." A few weeks later, the unthinkable happened. After getting home from school, I walked into the house, and my mother was sitting at the kitchen table. Her eyes were swollen and red. She broke the news to me, "Your dad died today at work. He had a heart attack." I began to yell and tell her she was not telling the truth. True enough, she was. I ceased to understand why my dad died. I felt like someone had stolen my heart out of my body and stomped on it. I was devastated. I never imagined life without dad. I mean, I was daddy's girl. Was I not enough?

I lacked clear knowledge about God at the time except that he brought people to heaven when they died, so I did not blame Him. As a seven-year-old, I wanted someone to blame, so I started to blame my mother. I internalized the thought that my mother was the person to blame for my father's heart attack. She had to have done something wrong. I shut down. Everything in sight just seemed wrong. I felt like a part of me died with my father. I had so many dreams that I wanted to come true. So many more trips to the store to look forward to, but not anymore. They were all gone.

    Day-by-day, gradually, I started to function again. I thought if I got back to my normal activities, maybe I would wake up from this bad dream, and my dad would come back again. If I did everything, he told me to do, I would be close to him again. At an incredibly young age, I pushed the pain into a figment of my mind and substituted the pain with accomplishments.

I tried to remain normal, but every time I would see other kids with their fathers, something in me would just strike every emotion. I would feel anger, rage, jealousy, sadness, etc. A moment that I thought I was away from continued to follow me. Blaming my mother became the norm for me. The more she tried to help me, the more I rebelled. I felt like she hated me. I started to hate myself. Later, I released the blame from my mother and assumed responsibility for it. I figured it was my fault. I thought I worried dad to

POSITIONED

death by asking for a bookbag. Why did I worry dad about that bookbag? Maybe If I had just been happy with what I had, everything would be the same, and daddy would still be here.

Troubled

I was born and raised in Patterson Court, located next to Alabama State University. Patterson Court was a housing project for low-income families. To outsiders, it was viewed as a ghetto, poor neighborhood, or a place not to visit, but to us, it was a great community of people that cared about each other. Yes, we had normal issues, neighborhood fights, and drug dealing occur, but it was a place that we were proud of and never wanted to leave. Inside the community, you could get into arguments or neighborhood fights with other residents but stick together when outsiders tried to bully you.

I'm not sure how I had time to rebel and do unapproved things because I spent a lot of my time at the community center. The community center was the place to go. We visited it daily. During the summer, we were served lunch, participated in many programs such as 4-H Girls Scouts, Camp Sunshine, African Dance Class, and listened to motivational speakers. A lot of the speakers are still stuck in my head to this day like, "Think Big When you are up or down, think big when others decide to frown, think big, think big, oh think big, think big…" Only people from Patterson Court can reference the "Think Big Man" and song, lol. The best part of the community center was the dances on Friday and Saturday nights. Each week, we saved our one-dollar allowance to attend the dance. We practiced our dance moves all week.

    The center director was viewed as a role model to us. We had tutoring classes at the center and later became tutors for others. The center was designed to prevent youth crime by providing a safe place for youth to gather and participate in extra curriculum activities that encourage good decisions. During the Christmas season, a very generous church would allow us to make a wish list. The week prior to Christmas, the church members would deliver the gifts to us. I was overwhelmed with their generosity. Our parents always purchased Christmas gifts for us, but this was an extension of kindness. In my teen mind, I thought the church members were rich. I vowed one day I would do this for a child.

    I remember the center director appointing me as devotion leader during our weekly Bible study meetings. I still have the award to this day. Despite all the activities offered at the community center, I still managed to desire the streets.

    One day at church, I decided I should go up to be baptized. Surely, God was the answer, and everything would change for me. I answered the questions: *Yes, I believe Jesus died on the cross for my sins. Yes, I believe that he lives. And yes, I believe that he is coming back again.* After this, I felt good, but right after the baptism, I felt the same way. The hate, guilt, and blame still resided inside of me. When my mom started being strict on me, I thought she hated me too. I did not understand why I had to be in the house at a certain time, could not go certain places, or why she treated me as if I were better than the other kids in the neighborhood.

    I was forced to go to church and the community center. I went to school and made good grades but then snuck and did everything I was told not to do. I became a great actor. To my mother, I was a good child. I made A-AB honor roll every reporting period, was involved in several activities at the community center, and to her knowledge, did as she told me to do. Later, skipping school and disrespecting my mother became my reality. I would talk back, pout, run from her, and try to run away from home. For some reason, no matter what I did, nothing I tried could replace the loss I felt from not having my father. My thoughts were I had tried Jesus, and He did not do it. Nothing magically appeared. I needed to find what I was missing. I started to find new interests and figured maybe I just had not tried enough. If I

POSITIONED

continued to search the wild side, something would give me that feeling. My desire became deeper and deeper. Then it hit me. Maybe I should try doing everything my dad did. Surely, that would make me closer to him.

The Crave

Entering late teen years, I began minor alcohol consumption and partying. At first, it seemed like I was living my best life. But after a while, my actions just became routine. I thought for sure alcohol and clubbing would give me what I felt I was missing. What started off as an infrequent activity progressed to frequent occurrences. I thought, what am I missing? Perhaps, it is the boy I am supposed to be with. Being a young, thick-in-all-the right places, chocolate girl from the projects with a dollar sign engraved gold tooth, I always had a thing for "bad boys". Accustomed to the southern hipped era I grew up in, I was attracted to this type of guy and in turn this type of guy was attracted to my "banging body". Surely, if this is the type of guy I always attracted and desired, this is who I needed to date. The sad factor is that many respectful, hardworking guys expressed interest. With insecurity, I failed to receive their advances of interest to be sincere.

I dated guys that I thought would fill the emptiness I felt. The more money the guy possessed, the more attracted I was to him. I was neighborhood-groomed with the idea that if I were a good girl, I could turn a bad boy good.

POSITIONED

Like in the movies, the good girl always turned the bad boy good. After all, I was proud of the neighborhood I grew up in and would be ready to set the record straight with anyone that spoke against it. At this point, I had three things that I was trying to fill the pain with—alcohol, clubbing, and dating bad boys.

Not long after entering a relationship with a guy that was opposite of my normal attraction, I became pregnant. I guess I was indirectly asking for it because I never used any type of birth control. Out of fear, I refused to ask my mother about birth control.

After becoming pregnant, I thought, hey, this is the answer to my issue. I just need someone to love and make me feel loved. Although I hid the pregnancy from my mother for five months, I started doctor visits at five weeks. When I gave birth my senior year of high school, I cried my first tears of absolute joy. This was the first moment I did not think of myself. I was in disbelief! I thought I have a baby. OMG, I have a baby! This was indeed the best day of my life. I had a new focus, a baby boy. I thought God did this to me to slow me down and give me something to work for.

Shortly after graduating high school, I started to have a new desire, to have a complete family. I was willing to give up everything to be married and raise my son with both parents in the home. During this time, I was introduced to a holiness church. I started to attend the church with the hope that everything would go the way I planned. On my first visit, I received a prophetic word from the pastor. The pastor stated that I would travel all over the world and visit different countries, but the devil was trying to kill me before it happened. This terrified me as the pastor told me things I had never shared with anyone. I decided to go all in. During this visit, I received the gift of praying in tongues. To me, the prophetic word was confirmation that my happily-ever-after would come true.

     After being engaged to be married for a year, I finally came to the realization that the complete family thing was non-existent and would not happen. I lost hope and stopped attending church. It was only a figment of my imagination, and good things never happened to me. Feelings of abandonment and insecurities flooded my mind, body, and soul. I felt so low that I could not get back up. I went through months of questioning my existence. I was so hurt and embarrassed that I did not leave my home. I rapidly lost twenty to thirty pounds, and people started to ask if I was on drugs. After several encouraging conversations with my oldest sister, Felicia, and accepting a job to keep me occupied, I decided to press forward.

My desire for alcohol and clubbing was back. It greeted me by saying, "Girl, you are tripping. We are what you need. Forget everyone. Never love or open to anyone again. You are not worth any of it. You are not worthy of anything good." The job I had happened to be the only job I was consistent with, although I quit three times on the first day. Thankfully, my sister was a supervisor there, and each time I walked out, she followed me and encouraged me to come back.

I continued to think there had to be more. Nothing I tried was the answer to what I was missing. Life happened. I was a single parent that wanted to give her son the world but enjoyed drinking and partying. In my mind, it was okay if I always put my son first. In search of more, I started to seek success. I started college at Troy University. At the time, I did not qualify for Federal Financial Aid Assistance, so college was short-lived. Working full-time, attending night classes with a toddler, and paying out of pocket was not the ideal life. It was devastating. As a result, I began to dream and fantasize about my ideal life. I would write fictional stories as an escape from my situation. I mean, who dreams of having to feed their child noodles as a dinner meal. Determined to make it and not become a minority statistic, I chose to enlist in the military and serve as my dad served. I gained gratitude for my current condition and started to enjoy the journey.

  This journey included more partying, drinking, working, attending college, and jumping from relationship to relationship. The validation that I was receiving was stimulating and intoxicating as I was addicted to the approval of others. I became known as "Sexy Black" and "Baller" to my friends. I was that chick that was going to drink the best liquor, dress to impress, and hit splits dancing in the club, curse on the microphone, forget everything that happened, and laugh after hearing about it the next day. The girls I befriended did the same. We would take turns buying alcohol at the bar and then really need every dollar spent the next day.

  I hosted all-you-can-eat-and-drink parties. The parties started out as ways to profit but later turned into free events. The more parties I hosted, the more hostile I became. In reality, I hated the parties. But my thirst for validation was stronger.

  After years of this routine behavior, I wanted a way out but did not know if it was possible or how to do it. I felt obligated to serve others. Seeing smiles on the faces of others gave me strength and motivation to continue the partying. Success came, of course, but there was a cost attached which consisted of many sacrificial actions, lost time, frustrations, depression, increased alcohol consumption, more unexposed insecurities, and still an unfilled spirit. I mean, here I was successful, with a house, nice car, extravagant vacations, college degrees, a great career, with an intelligent, well-mannered son, and still, there was a feeling that something was missing. This thing called life had brought me so many disappointments. I tried everything. I was raised in the church. I went to church. I raised my son as a single mother.

    I had endured so many disappointments and such great pain that continued to pierce my entire body that I kept bottled up in the back of my mind. My thoughts were discouraging to the point that even they were incapable of being lifted. I had accepted many lies. This was it for me. I tried everything, and nothing seemed to work. I cried to sleep repeatedly, asking God, what am I missing? The thunderstorms of life continued to cloud my vision. This dark cloud hung over my head, and regardless of what I did, it remained there. On the sunniest, brightest day, my heart was dark.

Transformation

After returning from a combat deployment, I was invited to a party by one of my childhood friends. The friend and his Air Force buddies hosted annual weekend reunion events to meet, greet, and catch up on life. I had been attending those events since they started in 1998. That weekend was much different. I tried hard to get the vibe going. I drank so much alcohol that weekend. One thing was different. My friend did not drink with us. He was very mellow and chill. He looked so happy, and I could not understand what happened to him. At the close of the weekend, I finally messaged him to ask what happened to him and why he did not drink. He stated, "I stopped. I found something greater than drinking." He continued, "I weaned myself off alcohol. I went from liquor to beer to wine to nothing." It blew my mind! Finally, I was able to witness someone turn from alcohol! Never in a million years would I have thought that this friend would ever stop drinking or even want to stop drinking. He found Jesus. He found himself.

    At that moment, I made the decision to stop drinking alcohol. I'd like to tell you I stopped and never returned. I did not. I thought it was something I could do on my own. The truth of the matter is it was something I could not do alone. I started to drink again. My thoughts were that I was not made for anything good. I will continue to exist and do things my way. Once I slipped back into drinking, shame, guilt, and self-pity covered me. I began to drown myself in the sorrows of life. I had so many things I could not tell anyone. I had daily struggles with sleeping because of nightmares I could not tell anyone about. There are so many stigmas placed on people post-combat that experienced nightmares and readjustment issues. Alcohol becomes a coping mechanism to aid. What I do know is that God is strategic. When you tell him to stop you or change you, something happens. It may not be what you have in mind, but it will definitely be something to stop you in your tracks.

      Life happened. I made some of the worst mistakes of my life during this period. At the time, I felt like I was being punished by God. I could have blamed others and not accepted accountability for my contribution. Justice was not served. There were many ways that the mistakes could have been avoided or demolished. I just wanted it all to go away, not thinking of how the process would affect me later in life. Because I was raised and trained with the concept of accepting responsibility for my actions regardless of the consequences, to be a leader, and to carry others' loads, I put the mistakes in my rear-view mirror. When I did this, things started to shift. In conjunction with being the talk of the town, I found myself hiding from society. Somehow, I knew this was the answer to my prayers.

    Message to reader: If you are struggling with an addiction or stronghold, you have the power to stop. God has already equipped you with the power. Just decide to do it. When you do it, you will have to surround yourself with like-minded people. If you do not surround yourself with like-minded people, falling may be easier. Accountability partners help. When you decide you want to stop, going all-in is the only way for you. Finding purpose will solve it all. A great mentor once told me that when I find my purpose, alcohol will not matter anymore. The mentor was right.

POSITIONED

True Love

Darkness was so close to destroying me. One day, I poured my heart out to a close friend and told her everything that was going on in my life; how I felt like a failure, and nothing seemed to work for me. She gave me a book to read by a famous pastor. The next day, my heart was so troubled that I did not get out the bed. I grabbed the book and started to read. I could not stop reading this book. I cried, sobbed, screamed, and entered a relationship with Jesus all at the same time. I learned so much in this book. I had no idea that every time I had premarital sex, I was allowing others to enter my soul. I did not know the gospel of grace.

After all those years of trying to find what was missing, it was slowly coming to me. I started to see the light. I started to love myself, spend time with God, and every struggle became easier to overcome. I fell in love with Jesus! It was so effortless. To be close to Him, I read his word and spent time with Him. He did all the work. Chains and curses that had me bound no longer held me. I was free. My faith was restored! I was ready to soar. Now, I understand the reason I always felt there was more to life than what I was experiencing. Jesus is endless, and there is so much of him to explore. As a follower of Christ, He designed me to continue to seek Him and crave his presence. God said His grace is sufficient, and He shall supply ALL my needs. In the moment of surrender to God, everything was made whole. I became a new creation.

After falling in love with Jesus, I started to love me. I started to challenge myself by accepting new hobbies. I went to the movies alone, during the day, of course. I went to lunch alone. I treated myself to spa days, hosted paint parties, learned to ski, horse-back ride, and started reading books. I even hosted a book club. Because I had fallen in love with Jesus and myself, I could get to know myself in a new light. Wait a minute. I started to like myself. I started to enjoy my company.

Message to reader: To anyone that feels lonely, I challenge you to get to know you. When you know whose you are, who you are, and why you were created, you start seeing your value. You start setting standards, and you do not compromise out of desperate measures.

Lonely Road

In movies, the ending often entails the person that transitioned for the better receives applause, and everyone is happy for them. In reality, that is not the case. Transformation is a lonely road. People remember you by the identity created by your past mistakes and tend to remind you of those mistakes during your transformation. Unbelievers attach your identity to who you used to be, watch you closely to determine if the change has really occurred, and scrutinize your motives. After making the decision to accept a new light, I lost interest in the things I used to do. In search of defining my new identity in Christ, I lost the title of fun girl. I invited people to dinner and presented opportunities to indulge in new experiences. Several invitations later, no one appeared interested. The need for acceptance started to slide into my thoughts again. I had to make the decision to turn back to the familiar or keep rolling down this lonely road. Going down the lonely road became more enjoyable.

After taking time to get to know me, grasping my God-given identity, and un-attaching the identity placed on me by the things I did, life became easier to manage. This season allowed for a deeper connection with God. I prayed for God to add people of substance to my life. I started to build new relationships, served others, and participated in church small groups.

    Since then, my life has never been the same. No, I do not have it all together. In the small groups, I found many people experiencing the same issues. Issues that bring shame, guilt, depression, and anger. The beauty of a small group is the accountability partners, bonds created, and the realization that God created us to be in community with others. What appeared to be a lonely road transitioned to a season of love, laughs, and a community of supporting travelers to do life with.

When God Says No

During my military career, I developed an interest in becoming a warrant officer. Warrant officers are considered expert in their military occupation specialty (MOS) or branch. I started compiling a packet in 2010 after seeing a female warrant officer in Iraq. I thought it was cool that she did not have to carry a rifle. Instead, she carried a pistol worn in a thigh holster. Sad to say, but this was my initial motivating factor of becoming a warrant officer. The other reason was to be known as an expert in the Army and bragging rights. I wanted people to say, "She made it." Hearing that validation and words of affirmation gave me a high I never wanted to come down from.

At the time, I had no clue what it took to become a warrant officer. Warrant officers walked, spoke, and acted with such a prestigious demeanor that displayed no worries. Working to complete the prerequisites took a while but I managed to finish. To be considered for a warrant officer, each candidate had to achieve a General Technical (GT) 110 Score or higher on the Armed Forces Classification Test (AFCT), a test equivalent to the Armed Services Vocational Aptitude Battery (ASVAB). The difference is the

POSITIONED

AFCT is the name of the test given after a service member has entered the military. It is usually taken to increase scores to become officers or change MOS. After six attempts at the AFCT, I finally achieved the score requirement by making 112. I thought, "Wow! Finally, I will be a warrant." There were several obstacles along the way. At this point, I figured nothing is going to stop me now.

The recruiters enrolled me into the Warrant Officer Candidate (WOC) Courses. The recruiters obtained a position for me and scheduled me to attend the final approval board. Two days before the approval board, leadership retracted their support of my packet, including a moral-waiver request due to non-military incidents that occurred in 2006. At least that was the reasoning I received in an e-mail. During a phone conversation, a leader told me a phone call influenced the decision to retract their support. I was devastated. I tried everything in my power to change their minds. I challenged the decision with an appeal. It did not work. I was not granted an opportunity to appeal the decision. I went into a depression and a dark place that caused me to second guess everything. I wondered why God would bring me to this point to fail. I prayed from a place of bitterness and pain. If I am honest, this was not my first thought towards this issue. I was mad as hell. I wanted justice! I felt I was wronged, and wondered how my leadership could be so cruel, detrimental, and not see me for who I am. How can someone just call and ask someone to stop another person's dream and retract a decision that had already been signed off on and approved? After all, I was good enough to work at any level in the military on active-duty orders at any given time, only received the best annual noncommissioned officer evaluations reports (NCOER), and most reputable as being one of the best NCOs in the organization. I wondered why God would allow me to endure this and suffer from this hurt if he had forgiven me for my sins? Why is my past continuing to haunt me if I have taken a one-hundred-and-eighty-degree turn? I screamed and cried. I did not feel I could go on.

    I wanted to tell my leadership I was being punished for trying to maintain the struggles of the combat deployments I encountered. I wanted to tell them I was drinking excessively to go to sleep some nights, and I lost interest in many things when I returned from Iraq in 2004. I wanted to tell them during the times the incident occurred, I was still looking on the side of the road to check for roadside bombs and experienced nightmares almost every night from the fatalities of war. I wanted to speak my truth. I remained silent because the truth would have initiated a discharge. After all, the Army taught me to be resilient, no matter the situation I found.

POSITIONED

Finally, the need arrived to avert from victim to victor.

One day, I was listening to a reputable preacher on television. She gave a sermon that spoke directly to me. She said, "Have you asked God what he wants you to do, or have you told him what you want him to do?" The minute that I started to go into prayer about God's plan for my life, He started to show me He was not done using me in my current role. I realized I wanted to be a warrant officer to glorify me, to be boastful, and seek validation of others, not because it would glorify the kingdom's work. My reasoning for becoming a warrant officer was totally self-centered. I think it is amazing how God is gentle and patient with us until we seek His direction. The Holy Spirit said, "Okay, so you finally going to ask me what I want for you?"

Although the situation bruised my feelings, I gained peace in learning humility and knowing God had more for me. This experience influenced the decision to pursue a Doctor of Management Degree. I was content with obtaining warrant officer status, and God had plans of me becoming a doctor. Now, I find joy in knowing God blocked that position for me. Man cannot stop what God has already ordained! They were simply participants in God's plans for my life. No devil in hell can stop what He has for me! His word will not return void. The best part of this situation is that my finances were unaffected. I experienced an influx of blessings.

    Psalm 23:1 says, "The Lord is my shepherd; I shall not want." God will provide for his sheep. We MUST consult him and ask for His will? When He orders our steps, we must follow them. The despair and depression I faced remind me of the ultimate despair Saul faced in 1 Samuel 16:15-23. God's spirit departed Saul and allowed Saul to rule in his own strength. Saul chose to rebel against the word of God. Saul was severely miserable, depressed, and angry. Saul forfeited an opportunity to confront Goliath and achieve victory because he continued to rely on himself instead of God. In turn, David accepted the challenge and relied on God. David defeated Goliath! David put his faith in God. God was the source of David's accomplishment.

POSITIONED

Ignoring Gifts

Throughout my life, I have always had dreams. I never really understood why I would have dreams about people around me. The dreams would later come true. For years, I ignored the dreams. I thought something was wrong with me. One night, I called a guy I was dating several times and did not receive a response. That night, I dreamed about him and how he was living with a woman. I had never been to this guy's home. He lived out of state. The picture was so vivid and clear as if I were there. The next day, he returned my call. I shared the details of the dream with him. He was lost for words, started to stutter, and asked me where I received that information from. He hung up the phone and never called me again. At this point, I started to believe that there was purpose in my dreams.

Another time, I was having a rough time at work. I was under the supervision of a toxic leader. The leader made the environment so uncanny that I would enter the workplace early enough to pray over our section before anyone arrived. I would play gospel music at a low tone and placed a full armor of God statue on my desk. Each day I would be challenged with a different evil tactic. Prior to leaving work one day,

POSITIONED

I was working on an extremely pertinent task and I was given a deadline. After requesting an extension for the deadline or requesting to complete the project at home, the supervisor asked me to give him the unfinished project, and he would complete it due to my scheduled leave the next day. The Holy Spirit told me not to send it to the supervisor and that he or she was going to exploit me with it. I ignored the Holy Spirit and did what the leader demanded. That night, I dreamed about the situation. I saw the entire situation before it played out. I shared the dream with a close friend. I said, "If this happens, know that I dreamed this last night." I told her that I had not shared it with anyone else. The next day, EVERYTHING happened just as I had dreamed, EVERY single detail of the dream. I thought God was forewarning me so I would control my response and emotions.

There have been several times when I have had dreams about close friends and family. Called them the next day. Pray or encourage them with the message given in the dream, and they are overwhelmed with joy and always ask how I knew. I do not know why God does what He does. What I do know is that He is up to something. Whether the dreams happen to forewarn me, block mistakes, or help others, they are intentional.

I have always been able to look at people and read them from the moment that I view them. I would often tell friends, "No. She is not this, or he is that," etc. Often, I would be the only person that could see it. After getting to know Christ, I now realize that was a discerning gift, and everyone has not received it. I was often labeled as paranoid or a negative person. Before experiencing freedom, I was known for having a sharp tongue and saying whatever came up to whoever was on the receiving end. Many referred to me as the "clap back queen." If you came to me with something, you better prepare yourself for something that would hurt your feelings regardless of how tough you were. I was raised to be strong and not show emotions. The environment I grew up in would have eaten me alive if I had not. Not only was my tongue sharp, but my right fist was as well. Although I did not find joy in arguing a lot, I could do it with the best of them. The thing was, I was only going to argue for so long. I was never afraid to let my fist finish the argument. My thoughts were, I do not care who wins, but I am going out swinging, and I would never be afraid. Message to reader: The issue at hand was learning how to contain these actions. What I referred to as strength was truly weakness. Now, I know a strong person trusts in God and relies on the Holy Spirit to order their steps.

POSITIONED

Emotionless

Growing up without affection was normal in some families. I believe during slavery, many slaves relied on their strength to get them through and giving up would have cost them their life. They trained their children and families to endure the fight. Over the years, my ancestors taught strength and forced the idea of not showing emotions. I can remember hearing, "Stop crying, or I'm going to give you something to cry for." I can also recall saying the same statement. The lack of crying produces hardness. When your heart is hardened, emotions have no-where to go but out. When emotions are forced out, they are hard to control and may show up in verbal or physical abuse. It can even go a step forward and block your ability to communicate with others, shut down, or produce insecurities.

    As a kid, I never really heard I love you. When the first boy told me he loved me, I took it to heart, literally. My first time hearing I love you from family was when I left for my first deployment to Iraq at twenty-three years old. I always knew my mother loved me by the things she did to take care of us and all the sacrifices she made. I am not bashing my mother. She did far more than I could have ever imagined. Truth be told, I am unsure how she did all she did for us. I put her through hell. Her willingness to put up with our mess was evidence that she loved us. I did not know that hearing it would be so important.

      As parents, we take our childhood experiences and alter them to ensure our kids have a better life. At least we think we are changing it for the better. From the time my son was born, I tucked him in bed every night, read a bedtime story, encourage him daily, and told him I loved him. I never wanted him to go through life without hearing and knowing he is loved. One of the greatest accomplishments I have received is learning how to love and receive love. Now, my entire family and I say "I love you" each time we speak or see each other.

Message to reader: Say "I love you" every chance you are allotted to your spouse, children, family, friends, strangers, and enemies. Sowing seeds of love demonstrates the acceptance of God's love for you.

Grieve No More

As individuals, we are not taught how to deal with grief. I experienced grief at a young age. Some parents may argue that a child does not know what love is at that age, and it is impossible to suffer loss as a child. The truth is grief can be experienced with death or disappointment. Experiencing the loss of my father, failed relationships, brokenness, heartbreaks, and unlaunched dreams were all forms of grief. I was blown to know there are five stages of grief: denial, anger, bargaining, depression, and acceptance. I experienced all five stages in every obstacle faced. This is one of the times when people may say confidently, "If I had known then what I know now, things would have been different." Honestly, I cannot attest to that statement, although the thought pops up seldom. Overcoming grief has been the most fulfilling rollercoaster ever ridden. I did not find joy in the pain during the journey; it was found in the freedom of a relationship with Jesus Christ and the decision to forgive.

POSITIONED

Forgiveness

Forgiving others is key to moving on. I had to forgive everyone that hurt me in the past. I had to decide to love others the way that God loves them regardless of what happened. Colossians 3:13-14 states, "Bear with each other and forgive one another if any of you has a grievance against someone. Forgive as the Lord forgave you. And over all these virtues put on love, which binds them all together in perfect unity."

    Making the decision to forgive everyone that had wronged me has been the HARDEST yet MOST rewarding action taken in my life. Letting go of past hurts, disappointments, rejections, and fears are the keys to the freedom God provides. After letting it go, making it go, and locking the door, I experienced freedom from everything. Hate, anger, and bitterness left my soul and transformed into compassion for everyone that had ever wronged me. I began to reflect on all the mistakes I made in life. I decided if God forgave me, I must forgive.

    I was able to look people in their eyes that hurt me, extend a vibrant smile, and render the greeting of the day. Message to reader: You see, repaying evil for evil creates more drama. You want to make your enemies mad, repay kindness for evil, and watch God work. I am new on this journey and will need much mercy and grace as I travel on it.

Reflecting over my journey, I realize God is a strategic planner with intentions. When it is time, he will let you know. Jeremiah 29:11 (NIV) states, "For I know the plans that I have for you "declares the Lord", plans to prosper you and not to harm you, plans to give you hope and a future." Fulfilling God's purpose requires all of you. The way to get over a bad past is to create an amazing future.

Everything the enemy presented has worked for my good. Philippians 1:6, "Be confident of this, that he that began a good work in you will carry it on to completion until the day of Jesus Christ." On this journey, I was craving something that was a word away. Jesus said if we invite Him into our hearts and confess, He is Lord, we are saved. When we invite Him in, we are invited to experience the overflow in his Holy Spirit and grow with it. Message to reader: My friend-reading this book- instead of following your dreams or goals, try to focus on God's purpose for you. Start to speak and listen to him. He will guide you. Enter the kingdom of God, by meditating on Jeremiah 29:13(NIV) that says, "You will seek me and find me when you seek me with all your heart."

    I pray that your craving for Jesus becomes so profound that you allow the Holy Spirit to pour in you to make a difference in the world. When you have those challenging days, and you do not know which way to turn, turn to Jesus Christ by casting all your cares upon him, read your word, connect with fellow believers, and replace the lies with the truth of the holy word. You have the victory! He will position you.

POSITIONED

CURTISHIA WILLIAMS STARLING

Test to Victory

There have been many tests on this bumpy journey. The tests were an intentional part of my testimony. Without the test, the victory would be purposeless. Everything that God has allowed me to endure was intentionally designed for me to be victorious. The key to victory is allowing God to position you through the tests of life for His purpose.

Here are a few victories achieved from the tests during the journey.

Test: Teen Mother

Testimony: The enemy wanted me to be a statistic and to control my seed. God gave me the strength to raise a respectful, intelligent young man that is following Christ, graduated high school with an advanced diploma, biomedical science major, is currently pursuing a master's degree, and plans to obtain a Physician Assistant degree.

POSITIONED

Test: Loss of Father

Testimony: God has a place in heaven for all that accepted him. God is a Father to the fatherless.

Test: Premarital Sex

Testimony: God has shown me what it looks like to do it His way and why it is important. It is never too late to do the right thing. We can always repent, which means go the other way. We can have the promises of God. The only way to true happiness is in a relationship with God.

Test: Frustration of Failed Dreams

Testimony: Direction to God's purpose and identity.

Test: Depression, Anger, Pain, and Unforgiveness

Testimony: Freedom, forgiveness, and fruit of the Holy Spirit.

Test: Serving Others with Alcohol and Partying Reason that I Liked to Entertain Others

Testimony: The enemy was distracting me because he knows God gave me the passion for serving others in the kingdom. It is so fulfilling to see others smile because they are free from the strongholds of life and have grasped the promises of the Lord.

Test: Love for partying and clubbing

Testimony: The enemy wanted to distract me from praise and worship.

Test: Cursing on the Microphone at Club/Parties

Testimony: The enemy wanted me to think I was not good at speaking or I could not speak without vulgar language. It was a distraction from professing God's word and mentoring others. God knew I would have a career in speaking to others.

Test: Failed Relationships

Testimony: The enemy knew I would not be emotionally available to people. I would continue seeking to fill the void the wrong way. He knew I did not love myself, and I did not know my worth because when I came to know myself, I started treating my body like the temple of God and did not settle for less. God gave me the best husband I could have ever dreamed of.

Test: Disrespecting My Mother and Being Disobedient

Testimony: The enemy knew if he could keep us apart, I would not see how much my mother loved me, and I would not repent and tell her I was sorry. Once I realized the disrespect, I apologized, and now we are closer than ever. I went from being the worst child of six to being my mother's caregiver and ensuring she has everything she wants or needs.

Test: Drunkenness

Testimony: It has been replaced with alertness, expanding knowledge, helping, and serving others. The need and want of the taste of alcohol were removed.

CURTISHIA WILLIAMS STARLING

Test: Bragging, seeking validation, and telling goals to others

Testimony: Learning silence has been such a great experience. Instead of blabbing about everything I plan or want to do, I just do it. I pray about it and find joy in revealing the actions that God influenced to people around me. When working on things, I recite Isaiah 30:15, "In quietness and in confidence shall be your strength." This reminds me that God is the only person I need validation from. He is the only person that can give it to me. He gave me purpose and a mission. He loves me and knows why He created me. My plans are not surprising to Him. He gave me the desire for the plans. One valuable lesson learned is I wasted a lot of time telling my dreams and goals, only for them to fail. When I keep quiet, God shows out and gets all the glory. The significance is in the confidence and faith of the surprise.

Planning to do anything, be quiet, and talk to God. If you share your plans and goals, envious spirits will arise. It hurts to know that more people wish to see you fail than see you prosper. I found that some people are happy for you until you exceed their level of success or happiness. This reminds me of the story of jealousy.
After defeating Goliath, David gained popularity and military success. Saul displayed schizophrenic behavior. Saul's attitude towards

POSITIONED

David changed from love to hate. Saul appeared jealous and afraid of David.

Redemption Prayer

Dear Lord, I thank you for your generous will to be in my presence. Thank you for loving me and extending unending grace and mercy. Thank you for dying on the cross for my sins and granting forgiveness. Thank you for keeping me from myself. Thank you for the freedom you have given me. Help me to link with you as I study and seek your word. At this moment, I join in a relationship with you. Lead and guide me. I accept all that you have for me. In Jesus' name, amen.

POSITIONED

Letter to Dad

Dear Dad,

There is not a day that goes by that I do not think of you. Though it has been thirty-four years since I last hugged or talked to you, I still feel your love and presence. I want to apologize for not waiting until I was twenty-five to date. If you were here to meet your grandson, Kwameh, I'm sure you would have relaxed that rule. Kwameh plays college football like you. I did honor your rule of thirty-five to be married. You would love your son-in-law, Everett. People say that girls marry their fathers, well, let's just say all the family can see the resemblance. Thank you for teaching me my worth at a young age and instilling in me the notion that I deserve the best life has to offer. To this day, potato chips and ice cream are still my favorite comfort snacks. I hope I have made you proud. I have served in the Army as you have served. I spoke to some of your classmates, and they miss you dearly. Madea did a great job taking me to church on Sundays and giving me money balled up in her fist. Mom smiles when she looks at me. I know it was difficult for her when you first passed due to my resemblance to you. Mom has done a great job raising us. I wish

CURTISHIA WILLIAMS STARLING

I could have gotten you some help. I can still remember pouring the water on your chest that night. You have lived a life of entertaining, protecting, serving, and loving others. Auntie Pearl has spent a lot of time with me over the years and treated me as her own. Aunt Dot has spent lots of time with Shun. I met Mona, and we have formed a bond that only your children can do. Thank you for that necklace and cross you gave me as a baby. Your grandson wore it as a kid, and now I will pass it on to his kids. Dad, I am so proud that you are my dad. I hope I am making you proud.

Love You Forever,

Your Cool-Loo

www.ingramcontent.com/pod-product-compliance
Lightning Source LLC
Chambersburg PA
CBHW071316060426
42444CB00036B/3084